ALL ♥ OUR LOVE

*A collection of children's sayings
compiled by*

NANETTE NEWMAN

Collins

I would like to dedicate this book, the fourth in the series which began with *God Bless Love,* to all the children who have allowed me to introduce their innocence, their perception and, most of all, their truth to a wider audience than their immediate families. Truth is always stranger than fiction and children dispense it so generously. So, to children everywhere, this book is for you — with my love

Nanette Newman

my sister keeps biting
our Dog

Peter aged 6

When you know my hedgehog

he has a wonderful
personality.

Emma aged 10

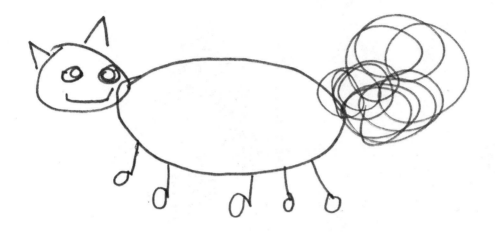

My Granddad says he doesnt
like women   So   we bought
Him a cat

Robert aged 8

my brother got marred   he
didnt fall in love he just
wanted some one older to talk to

Theo aged 7

I think love is borring.
people only do it when they
have lots of time off.

Una aged 10

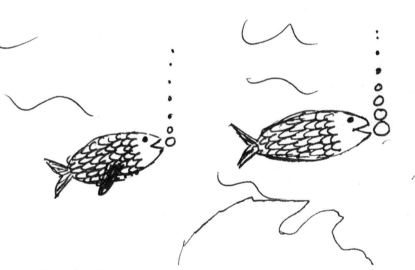

Goldfish are sex mamiaks mainioks

Shaun aged 9

Babies are born in hospital
some mummies bring them home
and some leave them there
for somone else.

Tracy aged 8

Babies are'nt very useful

Brian aged 6

A new borned baby can't talk it just thinks all day

Tina aged 6

My rabbit is the saddest person I know.

Carlo aged 8

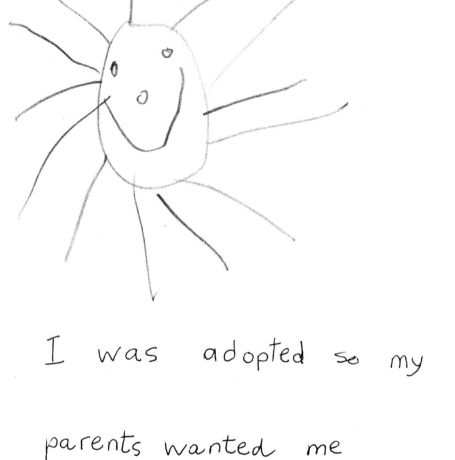

I was adopted so my

parents wanted me

very badly.

Lydia aged 8

Babies cry in the Dark becorse they thnk they havnt been born yet. Lorri aged 6

My sister carnt reed or rite and shes a literat

Paula aged 8

Our vicar makes little children suffer

Heather aged 6

I woodnt like me as a frend becorse I tell fibs.

Ann aged 7

Lots of people say they love children but mostly they're cross with them.

Vivien aged 11

at harvest festival God comes down and eats all the Food in the church

Melanie aged 5

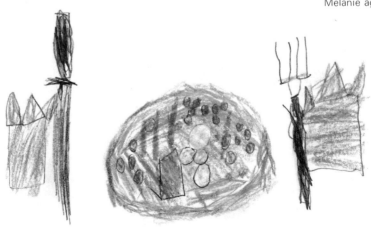

Our school cook is a
Secret Poisoner

Sam aged 10

Your parents have to tell you off
because they don't want you to
grow up like them

Simon aged 10

When my mummys cross
She talks with a
Nasty smack ●in
Her voice

Victoria aged 5

The man in the next
door flat has a bald wig.

Krista aged 9

My dad sais he's reading the news but he's only looking at Ladies with no clothes on.

Tim aged 10

My friend is Black and I'm pinkish. But we both have the same voice

Diana aged 6

every body you meet on holiday
are nicer then when you
meet them at home

Harriet aged 9

my daddy shouts when he speaks a
foregn language he doesn't know

David aged 10

theres not much ~~room~~
on the moon not even a
nice beach

Andrew aged 7

All the English people are never foreiners

John aged 9

I dont feel sad about peple deing in another langwige

Hyla aged 8

I went swimming but my body kept wanting to drown.

Jim aged 7

when your ~~dede~~ dead people tarlk about you alot.

Tracy aged 7

You have to have a funeral so that God knows your coming.

Astra aged 9

its not fair to blame God for everyth-ing becaus he can't answer back

Ruba aged 10

I went to my gran's
funeral to see her elated

Gavin aged 8

Jesus is too tired to come back
again he's gone off people

Sandra aged 9

theres nothing in the Bible
about sending christmas Cards

David aged 8

I wish god had ~~ritten~~ ritten
the Bibel so that evryone
coold understand it

Jean aged 10

I think Jesus would be
upset if he ~~kew~~ knew what
went on at Christmas!

Anthea aged 11

Jesus made his own bread

Pauline aged 6

Jesus wasn't very religuis

Una aged 8

I will be a teecher and get long holidays

Richard aged 6

. when I grow up I will be a doctor and Pull things out and Put things back

Linda aged 5

I ran away but nobody
came to find me so I
ran Back.

Mela aged 7

Old people and children need to be loved more than those inbetween.

Anna aged 10

I hate spoilt children because they have everything I want.

David aged 8

God should bless
ALL little children.

Sandra aged 8